tao paths
love

tao paths
love

MQP
MQ Publications Ltd

Contents

INTRODUCTION
TO THE
PATH OF TAO

On the Path of Tao each person is looked at as a microcosm of the universe itself. In this way we will see that, in looking at the subject of human relationships, we can see various aspects of the universe "coming into being," and being acted upon; and how each decision, each time we come into a relationship with another, and every action, affects a long line of people, energies, and emotional outcomes.

Taoism is not primarily a monastic tradition.
There is much to be learned from the ancient
masters, as well as a few contemporary ones,
about human relationships.

From the cosmic dance of yin and yang
through the art of the bedroom, and advice on
working with others and creating a vital and helpful
community, we will explore the teachings on this
essential, and important, subject of
human relationships.

The Path of Tao is one of wholeness, balance, and harmony. It began eight thousand years ago in China, yet the basic

principles continue to be used today. It is less a religion and more a *philosophy*. It is a way to work *with* change rather than *against* it.

The Path of Tao is the Path of least resistance, of going with the flow of nature (*wu wei*). It uses the metaphor of water, which adapts itself to the shape of whatever container it finds itself in, always flowing to the low places which, though soft and yielding, can over time cut its way through solid rock.

Lao Tzu, the great ancient sage of Tao, said that the Path of Tao is one of seeing simplicity in the complicated and achieving greatness in small things. It is a Path that respects, and even honors, the Value of Worthlessness and the Wisdom of Foolishness.

Chuang Tzu, a great sage of Tao, says, "Those who follow the Tao are strong in body, clear of mind, and sharp of sight and hearing. They do not fill their minds with anxieties and are flexible in adjusting to external conditions."

It is a way of life followed by the
peasant, the farmer, the gentleman
philosopher, and the artist.
It is a way of deep reflection and
learning from nature which is
considered the highest teacher.

The Path of Tao offers us a simple, practical way of being and living, a way of comporting ourselves on our journey between birth, death, and beyond.

In wonderfully illustrative texts such as the *Tao Te Ching* and *Chuang Tzu* we can find inspiration, illumination, and expedient advice on life, death, and all that lies between.

In Chinese medicine practices, we can find cure and comfort for many modern and not-so-modern ills and complaints. The practices of *chi kung* and *tai chi* can give us ways to stabilize and balance our bodies, allowing us to lead long-lasting and healthy lives. Taoist advice on sexuality and relationships can guide us gracefully through the difficult labyrinth of human sexuality. And through Taoist spiritual and meditation practices we may finally arrive at that precious point of power described in the Taoist tradition as Returning to the One—the source of our own being as well as being-ness itself.

The *Tao Paths* series offers quotes from the traditional Taoist works as well as jewels of wisdom from contemporary Taoist masters. Alongside these words of wisdom you will find stories to delight, mystify, and enlighten you in the deep layers of Taoist thought and practice.

Covering a wide range of Taoist tradition we will explore the ways in which the ancient sages as well as the modern masters have given us tools and practices to plumb the depths of our being and reunite us with our eternal source, the Tao itself.

Tao Paths, Love will teach how to maintain healthy relationships—emotionally, psychologically, and sexually—and how to study the relationship between ourselves and the natural world around us, and the infinite depth of our own internal world.

Tao Paths, Harmony teaches us how to be at one with the world around us.

Tao Paths, Long Life teaches how to achieve a long and healthy life and how to live fully in each moment.

Tao Paths, Good Fortune explores the realms of destiny, karma, and good fortune.

Today's problems are real and profound. They often seem unresolvable, and call for some remedy that can be applied to everyday life. The Path of Tao offers a way through. Its advice and wisdom is real, and eminently applicable, regardless of race, religion, or gender.

What the ancient men and women of Tao learned through countless years of observation and practice can be just as useful today as it was in the time of the legendary Yellow Emperor.

The Path of Tao is not just an ancient, foreign, mystical path; it is a cross-cultural, nonsexist, practical, even scientific way of viewing the world and our place within it. Its practices and philosophy work on many different levels—physical, emotional, psychological, and spiritual.

The beauty of the Path of Tao is that there is nothing to join, no vows to take, no special naming, or clothing style to follow. There is no reason to give up your own religion or culture to benefit from the wisdom of Tao. Its teachings can be applied on many different levels in many different circumstances.

In China, there are temples of Taoism, a religious form of Tao (*tao jio*), complete with priests, liturgy, and rituals. But the original philosophical form of Taoism (*tao jia*) was intended as a way of life.

The roots of Taoism go back thousands of years, the knowledge gleaned over the centuries can be just as helpful for the modern world as in the Tang Dynasty. Guiding us onto the path of least resistance and finding a way to work with the currents of change and renewal, and to feel our sense of connection to the sacred.

You will meet many strange and wonderful characters in these pages—from the lofty wisdom of Lao Tzu to the often ridiculous metaphors of Chuang Tzu to the down-to-earth tales of Lieh Tzu.

In between you will meet hunchbacks, cripples, lords and servants, wise sages, and foolish seekers after Truth. But pay attention, you may meet yourself here.

Taoism teaches us that all life forms exist in relation to all other life forms. Indeed, it may be said that nothing in the universe has its own intrinsic reality but exists only in relation to everything else in the universe. The Taoists do not view the world as a static form but as something that is continually coming into being. Not only that, but all parts of that world are coming into being in relation to all the other parts. They are, in turn, acting upon or influenced by these other "coming into being" things.

Relationships is a big subject. In this book we will be looking at Taoist views on, and practices in, human relationships—with each other, with family, with friends and loved ones, with marriage or life partners, and with one's larger community.

THE COSMIC
DANCE OF YIN
AND YANG

To the Chinese, the universe is divided into two polarities, yin and yang. In this way, all elements are paired and balanced with each other—night and day, sun and moon, moist and dry, dark and light, fire and water. It is through awareness and experience of this interdependence and interrelationship that the universe, and we humans within it, remain in balance.

The principle of yin and yang is fundamental to any understanding of Taoist philosophy, sexual yoga, or what we know of today as Chinese medicine. It is of prime importance in working with relationships, whether they are between two or more people, or even with and within groups of people.

The qualities of yin are darkness, water, cold, rest, inward and downward direction, stillness, receptivity, and what we think of as femaleness. The qualities of yang are brightness, heat, activity, upward and outward direction, aggressiveness, expansion, and what we think of as maleness.

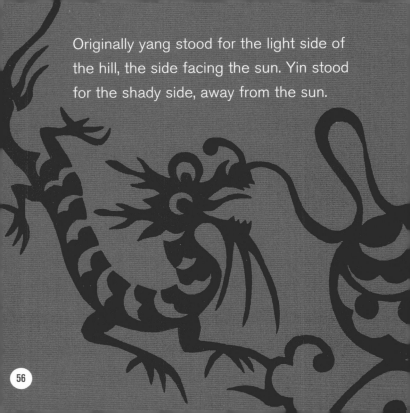

Originally yang stood for the light side of the hill, the side facing the sun. Yin stood for the shady side, away from the sun.

The ancient Taoists,
those natural
philosophers of
change and balance,
used the concepts of
yin and yang to
symbolize the
polarity of existence.

Everything that exists can
be assigned either to
yin or yang, thus identifying
its polar aspects.

Yin and yang each contain a piece of the other. Just as all males have a female aspect, so do all females have a male aspect.

There is no light that does not contain an element of darkness, and there is no darkness without its tinge of light, an important point to remember when dealing with relationships.

Yin and yang theory doesn't merely set opposites against each other. The well-known *tai ji*, or yin and yang symbol, one of the oldest symbols known to humankind and certainly one of the most powerful, shows the two primal forces of the universe, each enfolded within the other.

Yin and yang is the Way of heaven and earth, the fundamental principle of the myriad thing, the father and mother of change and transformation, the root of conception and destruction.

SU-WEN

This perception of existence as a vast and timeless ocean of spotless purity upon which, through the interplay of dark and light, the myriad illusions play like ever-changing cloud formations or restless waves, is of such immense antiquity that no one can say whence it first arose.

JOHN BLOFELD

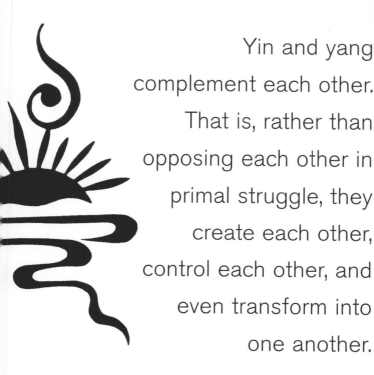

Yin and yang complement each other. That is, rather than opposing each other in primal struggle, they create each other, control each other, and even transform into one another.

They are as one and at the same time a division and a reunion, and if they are spoken of as contending forces, they are also cooperating powers and the tension in which they are held is that of harmony.

J.C. COOPER

Changes of every kind—from the transitory changes of state to deep-rooted fundamental transformation—are brought about by the active principle, yang, but it is the constructive principle, yin, that causes everything to assume a stable, concrete form (or cause to exist altogether).

MANFRED PORKERT

We all have both yin and yang qualities within ourselves. The balance of these two qualities is not static and concrete, but moving and shifting. At times our yin side asserts itself, at other times our yang.

No one aspect is right for every situation; it is best to recognize and be willing to work with the ever-shifting balance of power in any situation or moment.

The yin-yang view of the world is serenely cyclic.
ALAN WATTS

Innate instincts
belong to
yin while
acquired skills
belong to yang.

As everything in the manifest world, the realm of dualism arises from the relationship between the two polar opposites, the yin and the yang, it is the main concern of life to understand them and keep them in balance and harmony.

J.C. COOPER

Under heaven everyone knows that

the existence of beauty

Depends on the existence of ugliness.

Everyone knows the capacity of kindness

Depends on the existence of the unkind.

Existence and nothingness are mutually born,

Difficult and easy complete each other.

Long and short shape each other,

Tall and short rest upon each other,

Sound and music harmonize each other,

Before and after follow one another.

LAO TZU

In the world of reality as we know it, or, as the Chinese say, the realm of the ten thousand things, yin and yang help define each other, and in doing so help us discriminate one thing or quality from another.

The opposites have a vital need for each other, just as no human being can live fully without relationships. An attempt to do so is either to stagnate or to court mental and spiritual malaise.

J.C. COOPER

By being aware and sensitive
to the balance and subtle
shifts of our own yin and yang
qualities, we are better able to
make proper decisions and
conduct ourselves with greater
integrity and foresight in our
dealings with others.

One must ripen slowly. One day inner and outer will bound to be one and you will wake up.

WU ME

The single most important point
to remember about polarity is
that yin and yang energies are
not separate energies; they are
one and the same energy, but
with two different charges.

MANTAK CHIA

Yin and yang are not two completely separate forces. They are, instead, different facets of one unifying principle. In this way we can see that each of us also contains different facets or sides to our personalities.

An important point to remember about the yin and yang relationship is that things change. One day the world seems one way and the next it seems an altogether different place. But if we keep that in mind, then we can more easily ride the changes and not be ridden by them.

There was once an old man who had one son and one horse, both of whom he valued very highly. One day the horse ran away. His neighbors came over to console him. "Oh what great misfortune," they said.

The old man sat and smoked his pipe and only said, "We shall see."

Then, a few days later, the horse came back, accompanied by several wild horses. Again the neighbors came over, this time to congratulate the old man on his great luck.

Again he merely sat and smoked and said, "We shall see."

Then, a short time later, his son was thrown from one of the wild horses and broke his leg. The neighbors all came over, calling out, "Ah great misfortune!" but again the old man merely sat and, between puffs of his pipe, said, "We shall see."

The next day the army came through the village, rounding up all the young men to press them into service. But with his broken leg the old man's son was left behind.

LIEH TZU

Just like in the *tai ji* or yin/yang symbol, each male has a female side as does each female a male aspect. This can be helpful in a relationship. Yang can also be looked at as the dominant role and the yin as the submissive role.

Oftentimes one partner in a relationship takes the dominant or the submissive role at all times. This is not true balance. Instead partners should look to trade off roles at different times.

The yin power of passivity is more enduring than the yang force of direct action; the one has a controlled, sustained power, the other is quickly spent and dissipated.

J.C. COOPER

In Taoist internal alchemy the metaphors of the Green Dragon and White Tiger are used. The Green Dragon is the yin energy and the White Tiger is the yang. It is in the fusion of these two elements that the inner elixir or healing medicine is created.

It is often said that without the stabilizing
energy of the quiet yin that the fiery aggressive
energy of yang would have no place to spring
off from. This is also true in a relationship. It

has been described as "the power behind the throne." Oftentimes the ostentatious, showy type of energy depends on the solid backbone energy in the wings to support it.

Sometimes it can take a little work to discover the yang within our yin or the yin within our yang. But if we dig deep enough we can find that place in ourselves that correlates, energetically, with one or the other.

This can be important in a relationship. One should practice being a leader at times and a follower at other times.

It is in the natural attraction between the opposites that allows the Green Dragon in *li* and the White Tiger in *k'an* to be united. When the yang in the yin is united with the yin in the yang, the Golden Elixir of Immortality is produced. However, although the ingredients *are* inherently compatible, they need to be drawn out of hiding and gathered in a place where they can copulate and be harmonized.

EVA WONG

Uniting the outer male or yang with the outer female or yin is important but it can also be taken a step further. When the inner female of the male is united with the inner male of the female—then true magic is possible!

Not only that, but even with this attraction of opposites, each side must be "drawn out of hiding" and gathered together so that they can become harmonized. This is true union.

Here is a yin and yang practice
that anyone can do. It will teach you a lot about
yourself that you perhaps did not know before. For
one week or one day or even one part of a day,
practice making all your decisions and actions from
either your yin or your yang side.

You can play with working with different ones on
different days. If you see yourself as a primarily yin
person then make all your decisions and actions
from your yang side, even if it takes a bit of
imagination to do so. If you feel you are of a more
yang nature, take the other side.

This has nothing to do with male or female. There are plenty of yang-dominant females in the world as there are many yin-dominant males. This is entirely normal and natural.

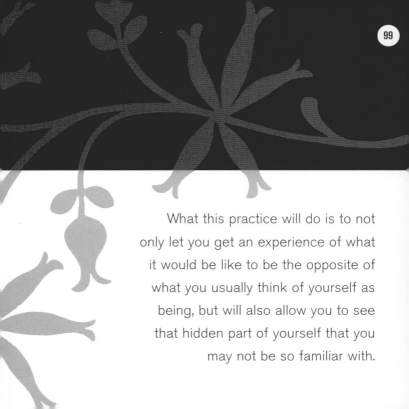

What this practice will do is to not only let you get an experience of what it would be like to be the opposite of what you usually think of yourself as being, but will also allow you to see that hidden part of yourself that you may not be so familiar with.

The spiritual value of relationship is to fulfill one's own obligation but not to have expectations of the other person.

HUA CHING NI

It is impossible to
be all things to all
people. It is equally
impossible to be all
things to one person.

The delicate interplay of yin and yang has a circular effect: A woman who is skilled at receiving and transforming will enhance her man's ability to give; a man who knows that his woman has been powerfully and happily affected by him becomes motivated to give even more.

FELICE DUNAS

Sometimes opposites can
complement each other.
Sometimes they attract,
and then again,
sometimes they repel.

This desire for union is inherent in all of us, but sometimes what we may think we are looking for in another person is actually something we seek with the divine! In this instance, there is no way that another person can ever live up to our expectations.

We cannot always be looking for someone else to complete us. That is too great a burden to put onto anyone and usually ends in frustration.

The principles of yin and yang suggest the inherent movement of the Tao. After all, life implies movement. In order to retain the flexibility that Lao Tzu talks about, we have to sustain the quality of movement in our lives.

This doesn't mean running around madly from one scene to another, one relationship to another, one religion to another, but rather something internal, an openness to change and new experience. It implies a dynamic engagement with life.

While there is no place in Taoism for a moral judgment on same-sex unions one still has to take into account the yin and yang balance. It is true that even in same-sex relationships there is often one partner who assumes the yang position while the other assumes the yin position.

It is important that if you are a male in a same-sex relationship, you still get some yin energy into your life, be it from energy practices, diet, herbs, or just allowing the yin earth energy into your being. The same is true for a woman in a same-sex union.

Stand or sit facing the sun, eyes closed to protect them. With your mind intent "inhale" yang energy from the sun down into your lower abdomen three to nine times. Feel this energy heating up your lower *dan tien* and then circulating throughout your body.

Stand or sit facing the moon, eyes open or closed. "Inhale" the yin energy of the moon into your lower *dan tien* in your lower abdomen three times. Feel the cool watery energy of the moon enter you, balancing all the hot centers of your body.

Instead of the battle of the sexes, we can use the yin and yang polarity as a way to experience that dynamic interaction as a concert of harmonious yet different notes.

LOVE

Humans have been trying for centuries to understand this strange attraction called love. It is something that brings out the best in us, and also the worst. It can take us to the greatest heights of ecstasy or it can break our hearts.

Traditional Taoist texts don't have a lot to say about love. You won't find stories about star-crossed lovers or directions on how to find the perfect mate.

To the Taoist, nothing exists of itself. All things exist in relation to something else. This vision of unity and joyful diversity can empower us to live a life of harmonious and exciting engagement.

When we say "yes" to love
we are saying
"yes" to life itself!

Love is a beautiful passion;
however, when emotional
force or possessiveness is
attached to what one loves,
the sublime state of
pure love is degraded
or damaged.

HUA CHING NI

No one can own another
person, either physically
or emotionally.

When we try to possess
someone else we end up
grasping emptiness.

Many people end up in relationships out of fear—fear of being alone, fear of being unloved, fear of being left behind, fear of growing old, and even of dying without company.

Many people view love as some sort of uncontainable, uncontrollable force of energy that explodes on contact.

In ancient China there lived a beautiful woman named Mi Tzu-hsia, who was the favorite of the Lord of Wei. At that time, according to the law, anyone found riding in the lord's carriage without his permission was punished by having their foot cut off.

Once, when Mi Tzu-hsia's mother became ill, she was so upset that she immediately set out in the lord's carriage to see her without consulting the lord. But when the lord found out he only praised her for her filial devotion.

"Imagine," he said, "risking such a severe punishment for her mother!"

One day while she and her lord were walking in the garden Mi Tzu-hsia picked a ripe peach and, finding it delicious, she gave it to him to finish. Again he praised her, saying how much she must love him to forget her own pleasure to share it with him.

Years later, as Mi Tzu-hsia's beauty began to fade, she fell out of favor with her lord. When she had done something to offend him he rebuked her, saying, "I remember how you once took my carriage without my permission. And another time you gave me a peach that you had already bitten into!"

HAN FEI TZU

Many people have the mistaken notion that emotional ties are subject to moods or whims. When they are in one mood their partner is the most wonderful person on the earth. Then, when they are not feeling so good, the other person is suddenly their worst enemy.

If love is true,
the experience
of love and deep
joy occur in the
same moment.

HUA CHING NI

Too many people look at love like a movie or a romantic novel.
Real and lasting love, like many a wise man or woman of Tao, is not outwardly showy.

How do we know when love is real?
Can we still love that person even
when we are angry with them?

Can we still love them even when we
have become accustomed to their
every bad habit?

Can we still love them even when
they no longer surprise us?

True love blooms, not only in our hearts, but in our very souls.

You know love when

your heart is open.

HUA CHING NI

True love, like the Tao itself, can be alluded to but never really captured. It can be described but never really explained.

Sometimes the only way we can truly know love is by its absence.

Or perhaps it is a certain indefinable something that makes us feel better about ourselves when we are with that person.

At sunset I come out of my door

And watch you walk by.

With your fine makeup and your

charming locks;

Your fragrance filling up the street.

YUEN FU

Love is something that calls out to us from the deepest part of our being.

A long night: unable to sleep.

The moon was so bright.

I seem to hear someone

calling. Into the empty night

I answer "Yes!"

YUEN FU

Love can bring out the best in us but it can also bring out the worst in us. It can inspire or destroy us. It can heal or break us.
It can give us joy, passion, contentment, and a reason to live.
It can also cause sadness, misery, and unfulfilled desire.

To say no to love
is to say no to life!
To close our hearts to love
is to cut ourselves off from
the very source of all life.
To be afraid of love is to
fear our very soul's most
secret desire!

Long ago there was a young man named Wang Chou who was in love with a young woman named Ch'ien Niang. They had grown up together and had often pictured each other in their secret dreams. But their

143

love remained a secret and so, when Ch'ien Niang became of marriage age, her father decided to wed her to one of his staff.

Wang Chou was heartbroken. He decided to go to the far off capital where he wouldn't have to see his love with another man. And so he trudged off into the countryside, shoulders slumped and tears filling his eyes. That night, as he slept along the river, he was awakened by the sound of footsteps and then someone breathing right next to him. It was Ch'ien Niang, who had run away to be with him! So they went off together and the years passed. They had two sons and were very happy with each other.

But Ch'ien Niang felt bad about how she had left her family and yearned to see them again. After all this time had passed they decided it would be safe to visit her family and so they went back to their village. When they arrived Wang Chou went to Ch'ien Niang's home first, just in case everyone was still angry. When he tried to apologize for Ch'ien Niang's unfilial behavior, however, her father said that Ch'ien Niang was there, lying in her room, where she had been ill for all those years.

"But she is back in the boat with her two children," said Wang Chou.

Her father did not believe him and so sent a servant down to the boat to see if it were true. When the servant reported back that Ch'ien Niang was indeed on the boat the sick girl rose from her bed, put on her jewelry and finest clothes and went forth to greet the woman from the boat.

It is said that when they met, their two bodies merged, each with the other and became one, fitting together perfectly, although there was a double suit of clothing on the single body.

CH'EN HSUAN-YU

Some people say *chi* is love. Some people say the life force of the universe itself is love. Love can be thought of as the attraction of yin and yang, or the way that yin and yang complete each other, even transform into one another.

Love can often conquer all mortal boundaries. When someone we love passes on, do we forget them? Do they not still live in our hearts and minds?

When our inner treasure is inexhaustible, we can provide limitless love and still remain independent and non-possessing.

HUA CHING NI

Meeting is hard. Harder is separation.

The east wind has no strength

And a hundred flowers wither.

The spring silkworm spins out death.

The candle's tears become ashes.

I sit before my mirror,

Sad that my cloud-hair will soon fade.

In the evening I chant poems,

And feel the chill of the moon.

LI SHANG-YIN

Discipline and mutual respect
between a man and woman prevent
arguments like a health regimen
prevents disease.

HUA CHING NI

Since we continually renew ourselves,

we do not fear losing love.

HUA CHING NI

The Valley spirit does not die;

It is called the Mysterious Feminine.

The gate of the mysterious feminine

Is called the Root of Heaven.

LAO TZU

Because it is empty, we call it
a valley. Because there is no
limit to its responsiveness, we
call it a spirit.

YEN FU

While it takes a combination of yin and yang to complete the circle, women, because of their intrinsic yin nature, have always been looked upon as naturally close to Tao, and better able to fuse the inner yin and yang to produce the Golden Embryo of spiritual immortality.

It was considered especially easy for women to attain the essence of Taoism even under the rigorous conditions of patriarchal society.

THOMAS CLEARY

Traditionally, women were considered to be inherently more spiritual than men and, therefore, it was easier for them to attain Tao. Because of their ability to give birth, women were considered more powerful than men. Sexually, woman were also considered to be energetically superior to men.

It is this reason that men have been both in awe and even, at times, in fear of women's inherent powers. It is because of this that men have often felt the need to oppress and rule over women for thousands of years. This explains much of the history of "mankind."

Know the strength of man,
But keep a woman's care!
Be the stream for all things
under heaven.

LAO TZU

It is only when men and women can come together with equal and mutual respect that a deep and long-term relationship can be possible.

A balance of yin and yang, of both aggressive and supportive energies, is needed for a successful relationship.

One female element
and one male element—
we call this the Way.

Anyone seeking perfection in another person will be disappointed. Anyone seeking perfection in a relationship will be discontented. Look to your own cultivation before judging another.

Having realistic expectations and desires will allow each person in the relationship to grow and thrive in a natural fashion.

Not to have feeling is inhuman.

To be carried away by feeling is foolish.

Not to have desire is death.

To be a slave to desire is to be lost.

DENG MING DAO

There is nothing inherently wrong with desire. It is only when we allow our desires to take over our lives in an unhealthy or unrealistic fashion that it becomes a problem.

If one desires to receive

One must first give.

This is called profound

understanding.

LAO TZU

When you love, love fully, love majestically, love dramatically even, but always stay grounded at the same time.

The Chinese character for love, *ai*, contains the sign for a person, under which is the sign for a heart. Surrounding this is an embracing hand.

The Chinese character for care, *quan*, contains the sign for an eye. Above this is the contraction of a sign that means to nourish.

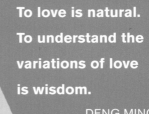

**To love is natural.
To understand the
variations of love
is wisdom.**

DENG MING DAO

MARRIAGE

Marriage is a subject which has mystified and confused people for many generations. What is a good marriage? How can we make marriage last? How do we know the other person is the right one for us? How do we deal with problems when they arise?

What we can do is take the basic principles of yin and yang, of how to conduct oneself in relationship to others, of how to use whatever situation in which we find ourselves as a form of self-cultivation, and apply all this to the subject of marriage.

We must ask ourselves, what is the marriage for? Is it so that two people can avoid loneliness? Is it because two people are so in love with each other they can't bear to be apart? Is it to produce children and create a family? Is it to form a partnership of the heart and soul?

When choosing a life partner it is best not to base one's decision on superficial things. Beauty will fade with age, health will decline, wealth can be lost, celebrity will go out of fashion. Make your decision, rather, on the intelligence of the heart.

One aspect of a good marriage that is often overlooked is compatibility. After all, you're going to be spend a lot of time together, if not a lifetime. Do you really enjoy each other's company? Are you inspired, interested, intrigued by each other?

To base a marriage on anything other than true heart love, respect, and mutual cooperation is to invite disaster.

A marriage could be seen as two countries, existing side by side, with interconnecting borders and a common, or at least similar, language. Of course there are sometimes feuds, misunderstandings, even boycotts. But as long as it doesn't escalate to outright war the marriage can work.

It is said that in marriage, even more so than in a monastery, one can find all the challenges and opportunities for self-cultivation.

When we look at marriage as an opportunity to work toward self-realization we will see it in a different light than merely two people living together who have signed a piece of paper that gives them permission to do so.

Why do a husband and wife sometimes secretly complain about a bad marriage but still get along? It is not the problem of the reality of the marriage that they are complaining about; it is the problem of some dissatisfaction due to imaginary projections and hopes that were not fulfilled by the partner.

HUA CHING NI

It is most important that a marriage or partnership be grounded in reality. It is simply not realistic that one person should be expected to fufill every possible need of the other.

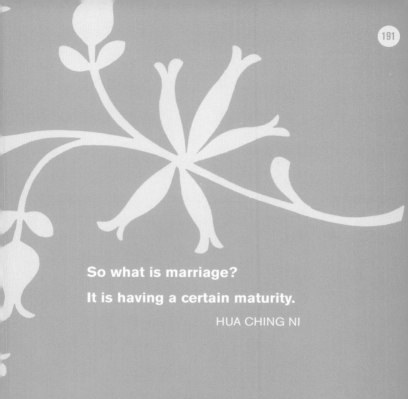

So what is marriage?

It is having a certain maturity.

HUA CHING NI

In ancient times, and in many different cultures, marriages were arranged. The idea of falling in love with someone first and then marrying them was foreign to most people. Marriage was seen as providing a partner to produce children and to help with the labor of growing food or maintaining a business or craft. If love followed marriage, all well and good, but it was not necessarily expected.

Often, people have unrealistic expectations of their partners. In order to stay monogamous one's partner is expected to be all things, from seducer to supporter. It is the inability of any one person to fulfill this role that leads to such a high rate of divorce.

Once you have acquired the awareness of others' flaws, you need not poke at every one of them. Sometimes, one compassionately ignores the chink in one's companion's armor. Constant awareness of human shortcomings can be a very gloomy way to go through life.

DENG MING DAO

If we view marriage as a spiritual agreement between two souls, we can be better equipped to weather the emotional storms that come up in every relationship.

What is a spiritual marriage? It can be anything from a relationship in which the couple pray or worship together to one in which each individual recognizes and respects the other's natural divinity.

It is not necessary to have the support or recognition of an organized religion to feel that you are in a spiritual marriage. That is between both of you and your own natural spiritual nature.

By creating bonds that
reach beyond this material
life we can create a true
and eternal marriage
"made in heaven."

A marriage based, at least in part, on spiritual agreement, will continue to grow and flourish long after you have both got to know each other in every detail.

Marriage, like spiritual cultivation, is made up of many small, unexciting moments. Unlike the movies, where everything happens in grand fashion, with swelling music and tearful close-ups, real life can be simple and dull. But it is in the constant flow of the simple and commonplace that real growth takes place.

A marriage based on a spiritual foundation will provide inspiration and instruction long after the initial excitement has worn off.

A marriage that is a true spiritual union will never cease to be interesting and challenging, and yet provide a sense of safety and assurance.

For many centuries in ancient China, the prevailing cultural tradition regarding love and marriage was Confucianism. This was a philosophy of order that put the Emperor at the apex of society, and descended in importance through the court officials, and, in each household, through the father and then through the sons. Only then, after the sons, came the level of the woman.

Under Confucianism, women, with their mutilated feet, were housebound and uneducated, and had no voice in politics, society, or even life outside their tightly-bound world.

In Confucian society well-bred women were trained to walk backwards out of any room in which men were present. They were trained to regard themselves as always being wrong in any dispute, and to feel themselves lucky to be spared severe punishment.

Taoism takes a different view from Confucians. Know the yang, but hold to the yin, says Lao Tzu. Know the important creative power of the yang but do not let go of the enormously creative power of the yin—the dark, mysterious, water womb of our origin.

With their emphasis on the yin, the essentially maternal, feminine energy of the universe, Taoists have always supported women's rights and privileges, even as Chinese culture became dominated by the inherently anti-feminine Confucians, followed by the puritanical Communists.

It is only when this balance is corrected and maintained that it is possible for men and women to come together in equality and harmony. It is in using the many energetic, emotional, and even sexual practices of the Path of Tao that men and women can create and sustain long-term healthy relationships.

While it may be hard to find many references to what we may think of as romantic love in the West, Taoism still gives us many guidelines and teachings that may be useful in today's often confusing world of love and relationships.

To make a
marriage last
both people
must grow,
both individually
and together.

A marriage based on mutual interests and a spiritual understanding, even if you are on different paths, will outlast a marriage based on mutual needs and unrealistic expectations.

Conflict can be a passion killer, but it doesn't have to be. It is both inevitable and necessary for the success of your marriage.

FELICE DUNAS

Conflict is inevitable. Anyone who doesn't realize that will never last in a long-term relationship. It is how we respond and react in conflict that will decide if the marriage will last or not.

Couples mishandle conflict by reacting with either extreme yin or extreme yang behavior.

Problems can be handled or often even solved by a variety of methods. There is no one method or technique that works for every thing in every time.

By taking the time to examine the energetic aspects of each situation we can then take the appropriate yin or yang approach.

Trying to outshout
or outsmart
our partner will
never work.

By applying the yin and yang principles of *tai chi* we can become better at arriving at a harmonious outcome when conflict does arise.

Harmony is the real
essence of marriage.

HUA CHING NI

Remember, even in same-sex relationships there is still an exchange of yin and yang energies. By being respectful of those roles and by paying close attention to the balance and harmony of each other's energetic and emotional states, you can build a strong and lasting relationship.

Allowing each other
to exchange roles
occasionally can give a
relationship new vigor.

A mutual exchange and sharing of ideas, thoughts, and feelings is the best way to build a relationship.

As we look around, we see other couples working
very hard at being couples, often taking the natural
swing out of their relationships.
Perhaps a thriving partnership is not built only on
special-effect romance and fireworks. It may
depend on not-so-special, day-to-day events.

CHUNGLIANG AL HUANG

Over the course of a lifetime, intimate partners move through emotional cycles of togetherness and separation. There are times when you can't stand being apart and times when you have to get away from each other. These cycles are a natural expression of paradoxical human needs.

FELICE DUNAS

226

If there is no harmony
between you the
marriage cannot last.
Or if it does it will be a
prison for you both.

Heavens above!
I want to love you
Our whole long life together with no ceasing,
Until the mountains fall down
And the rivers dry up.

When the winter thunders roar
And the summer rain turns to snow.
Only when heaven and earth merge
Would I dare to leave you!

YUEH FU

A marriage alternates between that of passion and love and the chilling times of tragedy, conflict, and adversity. An enduring marriage becomes like tempered steel.

DENG MING DAO

Over the years, we become rigid and stuck in our ways. Then, if one partner attempts to grow, or to try something new or different, conflict arises.

In the long run, marriage gives us the opportunity to grow, both emotionally and spiritually. It offers myriad lessons, countless challenges, and numerous occasions to reflect on our own desires, dreams, and visions.

Being successful in marriage is much like being successful in life. As the poet said: The love you get is equal to the love you give.

An old man and old woman had lived together for many years, given birth to three children, raised them, and sent them out into the world. Now they were alone, living on the edge of the forest in a little hut. It was very small and very simple and they themselves were very small and simple.

Over the years they pared their needs down so that their wants were very few and easily satisfied. They hardly spoke yet a look from one to the other spoke volumes. They slept, sometimes curled up together like two kittens, sometimes in opposite sides of the room.

They hardly did their breathing exercises any more. Instead they simply concentrated on each breath, each moment, as it unfolded within them. They walked a good deal, though without thought of any specified destination. Sometimes they sang together, songs that were old even when they were still young.

But most of all, they trusted each other. They trusted each other with their innermost secrets and they also trusted each other to still keep some secrets to themselves, like a buried treasure, remembered though hardly ever looked at.

They had lived together for a long time now and even so, sometimes they disagreed or even, occasionally, argued. But they had made a rule a long time ago never to go to bed mad at each other, though sometimes they lost a good night's sleep in working things out. But all in all, it was a good system.

And when they left this world of dust, one right after the other, they went easily and without fear. The lessons they had both taught each other in their long life together, along with their own deep spiritual work, had prepared them for the Great Transformation.

Many years later, some hikers came upon their little hut and found their bones there, intermingled, like branches of an ancient tree.

THE ART OF THE
BEDCHAMBER

The ancient Taoist view of sexuality is extremely different from modern attitudes about this most primal of human expressions. Instead of merely fulfilling sensual urges, Taoist sexual practices, called dual cultivation, show us ways to facilitate greater communication, and trust levels with our partners.

They also include aspects of health (physical, emotional, and psychological) and spirituality. Taoist sexual yoga is different from other tantric paths, such as those found in the Hindu traditions, in that it is simpler, easier to learn and use, and not as concerned with elaborate ritual and visualization techniques.

Taoism is concerned with the basic male/female attraction and interaction as well as the ability to use our own individual sexual energy to further ourselves in our quest for better health, a more stable and intimate relationship, and a greater sense of spirituality.

As with all Taoist arts, the Art of the Bedroom—or sexual yoga—is governed by cycles and seasons, by an awareness of our own energetic system as well as that of our partner. It is a way to tap into that energy and not only share it with our partner but direct it within ourselves.

Taoists cast no moral judgments upon the sexual act itself. Instead, they offer healthy and productive ways of being sexual, both within our own bodies and with those whom we love.

As far as Taoists are concerned, the only important distinctions regarding sexual activities are those between healthy and unhealthy habits.

DANIEL REID

The Art of the Bedchamber goes back to the ancient times of Huang Ti, the Yellow Emperor, that ancient, mythical sage-king who is credited with creating so much of Chinese culture.

The Emperor's teachers were three immortal women, who taught him the principles and practices of Taoist sexual yoga in order to satisfy his many hundreds of wives and concubines, and to do so without injuring his own health!

The Yellow Emperor complained to his three teachers that satisfying his many wives and concubines had so depleted him that he was thinking of forgoing sex altogether. But his celestial teachers warned him not to take such a drastic step.

It would not be correct behavior, they said, to abstain from sexual intercourse altogether. He was told that yin and yang have their activity and changes and that humans must not do anything against the course of Nature (*wu wei*).

By abstaining from intercourse the spirit has no opportunity for expansiveness, and yin and yang are blocked and cut off from one another.

CLASSIC OF SU NU

The Chinese have made an art, a yoga, a ritual, a therapy, and meditation of sex.

DOUGLAS WILE

On the Path of Tao sexuality is seen as a means of deep communication and communion between two people. It is not merely a physical act but a spiritual one.

To the Taoists, every part of life has its application for longevity, from diet to sex.

For thousands of years, the ancient Chinese were intensely interested in the links among sex, health, and longevity.

VALENTIN CHU

They experimented with means for greater sexual energy, which they believed was inseparable from better health and long life.

VALENTIN CHU

By having a better understanding of the energetic dynamics of sexuality, we can apply this knowledge to our pursuit of health, happiness, and wholeness.

The ancient Taoists discovered that it was possible to use human sexuality as a doorway into greater areas of emotional, energetic, and spiritual fulfillment. All it takes is a bit of patience, an open mind, and a deep level of trust and commitment from both partners.

Like the breath of life, sex is vital to the continuation of human beings. As a natural euphoriant, sex is vital to humanity's well-being. Unknown to most people, sex is vital to mankind's spiritual elevation.

STEPHEN T. CHANG

The Art of the Bedroom or the Tao of Sex is a way to use our sexual life to enhance and solidify our relationship with our partner.

The Taoists believed that the way to attain and keep physiological well-being was through proper application of the bedroom arts.

AKIRA ISHIHARA

In ancient China,
human love, expressed through
sexuality, was seen as the most
potent medicine you could take.
It was believed to cure most
ailments as it restored the flow
of *chi* which governs our vitality
and immune system. During the
Tang Dynasty (618-906 C.E.)
the Art of the Bedroom was
classified as a branch of
Chinese medicine.

Refining one's awareness of sexual energy—with or without a partner—is one of the simplest ways for humans to return to pure consciousness and experience the deepest rhythms of life.

MANTAK CHIA

On the Path of Tao sexuality is seen as a way to improve your health, help with longevity, and open energetic and spiritual centers in each partner.
Not only that but a healthy sexual life contributes to greater trust and communication between partners.

...if one partakes of all the various magic drugs and nurtures one's three natures, while at the same time being ignorant of the Art of the Bedchamber, those drugs and disciplines will prove to be without effect.

KO HUNG

Taoist sexual practices require a high level of sensitivity on both sides. Cultivating one's sensitivity not only heightens the levels of pleasure and response in each partner, but also sensitizes each partner to the other. It is not possible to practice Taoist sexual yoga without first cultivating this level of sensitivity in both partners.

The true joy of loving is an ecstasy of two bodies and souls mingling and uniting in poetry. Once a man has found an ideal partner he must try to make love to her ecstatically and poetically.

JOLAN CHANG

What exactly is this mysterious art? Actually, it's very simple. And, as with all Taoist practices, it involves balance, harmony, introspection, and naturalness. It also involves surrender, trust, and self-discipline, as opposed to self-denial.

Taoists advocate living in complete harmony with the great patterns of Nature, and they venerate womanhood precisely because women are by nature far closer to the primordial powers of the cosmos than men.

DANIEL REID

At the very heart of the Art of the Bedroom or the Tao of sex is the notion that woman is both energetically and sexually superior to man.

Know the male
But hold to the female.

LAO TZU

Woman is considered to be the repository of inexhaustible yin while the man is caught up in his all too quickly exhaustible yang. Applying this belief to other aspects of life, it also means woman are more often capable of sustained efforts, and are more conscious of long-term goals and effects.

Women, as yin, see sex as a way to communicate, share intimacy, and reach emotional depth with their partner. While many men also share these views, they also have the yang drive for physical release.

With the Tao, men and women can become true, loving, and equal partners, thus making the age-old conflict between the sexes a thing of the past.

JOLAN CHANG

Man is yang, fire, which is quick to flare up and also quick to burn out. Woman is yin, water, which is slow to come to a boil, but when it does it can continue in this way for some time. The secret is for the fiery man to learn how to pace himself to the watery woman so that they can come to a mutual boil together.

Think of the difference between dousing
a fire and waiting for boiling water to
cool off.

FELICE DUNAS

When he surrenders—the moment of sharing, the moment of yielding, the moment of physical and psychic attunement, with his partner as well as within himself—the man has the opportunity to expand both within and without to the greater moment, the greater union, the great attunement, to what we call Tao.

The term orgasm
does not appear in
the Tao. Its terms
are enjoyment
and satisfaction.

JOLAN CHANG

**One who retains his seed
increasingly respects
every form of life.**
MANTAK CHIA

One of the ways in which the Tao of sex is accomplished is when a man is able to put into practice the art of ejaculation control, or optional ejaculation.

How is this accomplished? As with all Taoist practices, it involves slowing down, paying attention, becoming sensitive to even the smallest of currents moving both within himself, and between himself and his partner.

Eventually, after much practice in sensitivity and mind and breath control, the man is able to stop ejaculation without physical intervention. At this point he is able to begin transforming sexual energy into spiritual energy.

In fact, men stand to gain even more than women from the practice; because it places them in a yin position, they may become more receptive to pleasure in general.

FELICE DUNAS

Cultivating sexual energy is important
in nourishing your spirit, but without
proper diet, exercise, meditation,
virtuous moral behavior, and love,
true cultivation is impossible.
Likewise, don't ignore sex and focus
excessively on the higher spiritual
centers; the roof will easily fall without
a strong foundation.

MANTAK CHIA

Besides contributing to a more healthy, energetic lifestyle, this slowing down process will give both the man and the woman the space to develop new areas of trust and intimacy, something that can be lacking in many modern relationships.

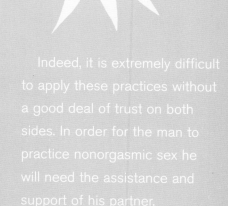

Indeed, it is extremely difficult to apply these practices without a good deal of trust on both sides. In order for the man to practice nonorgasmic sex he will need the assistance and support of his partner.

In the old days the times for a man to have orgasmic sex was strictly regulated by the time of the year (more often during summer, less during winter) and by his age.

According to the *wu wei*, or natural approach, it is better for each man to experiment and find his own rhythms. In this way he can keep his energy up, enjoy lovemaking as a longevity practice, and still not be too rigid and dogmatic about it.

Of all things that make man prosper none can be compared to sexual intercourse. It is modeled after Heaven and takes it pattern by earth, it regulates yin and rules yang. Those who understand its significance can nurture their nature and prolong their years; those who miss its true meaning will harm themselves and die before their time.

TUNG HSUAN

In the sexual practices of Taoism, there is a continued sharing of energy, trust, intimacy, and pleasure between both partners, and an emphasis is placed on the sage and healthy sexual practices that can build energy rather than tear it down.

Taoists say that it takes seven years to know the rhythms of a woman's body, seven years to learn her mind, and seven years to understand her spirit. How many men are willing or able to put in this kind of time to truly and deeply understand their partners?

Masturbation is a poor substitute, and we should treat it as a last resort when no love partner is available. To masturbate is a lonely endeavor, devoid of human warmth, contact, and communication. In the language of the Tao, it lacks the harmony of yin and yang.

JOLAN CHANG

If you feel unable to use your sexual power lovingly, then do not use it at all!

Sex is a gleaming, sharp, two-edged sword, a healing tool that can quickly become a weapon.

MANTAK CHIA

Too often sexuality is abused
in order to wield power
over someone else.
But this two-edged sword can
easily be turned on one's self.
This is not the way of Tao.

The role of the man in Taoist sexual practice is to serve the woman. The man should harmonize his mood with that of the woman.

CLASSIC OF SU NU

The ways of sexual intercourse are not especially strange. But you should be composed and at tranquil ease, esteeming harmoniousness.

A couple who can make love ecstatically together are likely to have provided each other with peace and harmony in every way and hence their lovemaking and attraction for each other may increase and become a more permanent one.

JOLAN CHANG

As a prelude to a session of lovemaking, couples in ancient China would do things together–read poems about nature, play music, watch a performance, stroll, converse over tea, play backgammon, or look at pictures. Such activities were considered important forms of foreplay, as they brought into harmony the thoughts, sense, and emotions of the lovers before they even touched.

FELICE DUNAS

Most marriage counselors
agree that, if the sexual life of
a couple is healthy then the
relationship itself benefits
greatly. And if it is not, then it
often spills over into other
parts of the relationship.

Taoist sexual practices can be powerful tools for a greater sense of well-being, physically, emotionally and spiritually. They also engender a high level of commitment and self-responsibility. The idea is not merely to become a great sexual athlete, or to use other people to enhance your own vitality.

These practices make possible much deeper levels of trust, communion, and communication than you ever thought possible. Use them well and you will be rewarded amply.

FAMILY

The earliest relationships in our life are with family. We are usually born into it, although some spiritual teachers tell us that we actually choose our birth family, depending on what life lessons we are looking for.

How can we be sure that the emotional bonds we form with our family can be nurtured, how can we continue our friendships into our later years, how can we raise our children to be whole and healthy individuals?

The basic pattern of cooperation relies on the correct organization of diverse energies. With this understanding one should not feel troubled about the differences that exist within one's family.

HUA CHING NI

Within the closest of families, there can be extremely divergent views on many things. But with mutual cooperation and mutual respect these need not become problems.

For most people, the family
is the first form of society
we experience.

Many of the experiences
we have with our original
family will create patterns that
will last far into our lifetime.

...the focus of modern
life has shifted from a
family-centered life to
a socially-centered life.

HUA CHING NI

Family life has changed immensely over the years, especially in today's often fragmented world. Family bonding over career, meals, and a shared outlook on life has radically changed. Often there is very little sharing within the family as social structures have shifted in the modern world.

How can we be sure that we are instilling the right values in our children, who are being brought up in such unsettling times?

Children today are bombarded
constantly with conflicting views
on sexuality, violence, racism, and
selfishness. Without the gentle
but firm guidance they receive
at home they will be lost.

Then again, many children today
don't have the opportunity
to spend time with their parents,
even if both of them live at home.
The need for mentors is crucial
for these children.

By instilling pride and a sense of self-worth in our children rather than blind obedience, we are equipping them to function in today's highly competitive and fast-paced world.

Be aware that your example carries through many generations to come. When instructing your children, example is better than precept.

HUA CHING NI

When we realize that our actions affect our children and even their children, we must learn to conduct ourselves as intelligently and virtuously as possible.

Even if we do nothing else of great worth in our lives, if we are able to raise healthy, independent, and loving children, we will have given a great gift to the world!

Family life is seldom smooth,
but its difficulties can provide
real substance for refining
one's nature.

HUA CHING NI

There are many kinds of families, from workplace relationships to our family of origin. Even monasteries are a type of family. The need for family is a very deep one in most of us.

We can create a
family of like-minded
people around us.
By doing so we will
be supporting our
growth and our
spiritual evolution.

Community is another form of family.
Creating community in our lives can
give us support and an opportunity to
share ideas, goals, and visions.

Very few of us can exist all alone. While it is true that many ancient Taoist masters lived for a time in the mountains, away from society—in order to pursue their spiritual cultivation without the distractions of the world—they usually returned to share what they had learned as hermits.

It is crucial for today's world that, not only do we share what knowledge we have gained through our spiritual explorations, but that we do it, as much as possible, while we are in the world.

The time for hermits is past. The time for grounded, highly individuated, "spiritual social workers" is here.

Learning to gain some self-control and self-awareness of your own is fundamental to being able to guide others.

People in the prime of their life are often very proud and arrogant.

Those who are physically strong like to show off their strength. You cannot discuss the Tao with them because they will not listen.

It is also useless to talk about the Tao with people who are young and immature. They will

not listen. If they do they are not emotionally balanced enough yet to appreciate it. Therefore, it is best to give responsibilities to those who are older and more mature.

Look for someone who has a clear direction about their life. They should have physical strength but must also have stamina and emotional stability. The key to good management is not necessarily in your own talent but in your ability to choose the right person for the job.

LIEH TZU

Your spiritual cultivation is not for you alone. Whatever advances you make will have profound effects on those around you, your family, loved ones, fellow workers, even society at large.

Alone on this night,

as the moon rises over Fu Chou,

My wife watches it alone.

Sorrowfully, I think of my son and my daughter,

They don't understand

Why I am far away in the capital.

The fragrant mist wets her hair,

The clear moonlight chills her jade white arms.

When will we be together again

To lean on the casement,

Watching the moon together,

Our tears drying on our cheeks?

TU FU

The Chinese word for good, *hou*, is a picture of a woman and child next to each other. The bond between mother and child is like that of the Tao itself and we are the children of Tao.

The softest thing
under heaven
Overcomes the
hardest thing
under heaven.

LAO TZU

When we are born,

We are soft and weak.

At death we are hard and stiff.

Young plants are soft and pliant,

At death they are withered and brittle.

LAO TZU

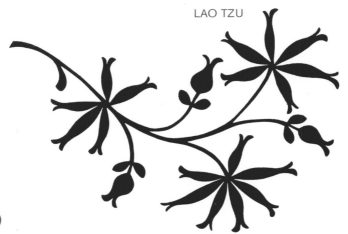

The Emperor went to the Taoist sage and asked him for advice on ruling the country.

"I have knowledge only about ruling my own life," said the sage, "I don't know anything about ruling a country."

"But I have a responsibility to manage the shrines of the royal ancestors," said the Emperor. "I also must conduct the ceremonies to give thanks to gods of the earth and sky. I wish to learn how to do all of this properly. I understand that it takes someone who can manage his own life properly before he can be expecting to manage an entire country. Likewise, if the ruler's own life is in turmoil how can he expect to be able to rule a country properly?"

At this the Emperor was pleased and went his way.

LIEH TZU

We must always look to our own faults, our own problems, our own internal dynamics before we begin to judge those around us.

It is often said that when we are with our family they tend to drive us crazy but when we are away from them we inexplicably miss them.

Respect and tolerance between generations is essential for a healthy society.

To care for others is to look after them.

DENG MING DAO

Once a man went out of his house wearing a white silk coat. While he was out it rained, ruining his coat, so he took it off and purchased a black one. When he arrived home his dog did not recognize him and barked at him. Angry, he began to beat the dog when his brother came out of the house and said, "Wait, you must not beat your dog. There is really no difference between you and he. Suppose that he had gone out as a white dog and come back as a black one. Would you not have been surprised yourself?"

LIEH TZU

Sometimes it is hard for family members to accept changes in us. Alternatively, it may be hard for us to accept the changes in others.

We cannot hold them in a set place. We must, instead, allow room for others to grow and change, even if we don't always agree with them.

LOVE AND
UNDERSTANDING

The old saying—you must learn to love yourself before you can love another—is true. Indeed, we can never even know another before we know ourselves. And we can certainly never understand another before we begin to have some understanding of ourselves.

Taoists use everything in their life for their self-cultivation. This includes their relationships, their health issues, their work, their suffering, and their joy.

In this sphere of life, under the conditions or law of polarity, we always feel good sometimes and feel bad sometimes.

NI HUA CHING

Once you unite all elements within yourself,
metaphorically referred to as the uniting of
male and female, the light that dispels
darkness appears.

DENG MING DAO

Men often exhibit yin traits such as receptivity and nurturing, and women have yang traits such as creativity and aggressiveness. Women are often proactive and men reactive; women can express themselves vehemently and men can respond passively and patiently; women can be adventurous and bold and men can prefer to sit quietly at home.

FELICE DUNAS

By going deep within ourselves we can find a sense of what it is that we seek in another. Then again, it is also of great importance for us to learn how to give ourselves what we need.

Remember, you are whole and complete just as you are. Take the time for self-cultivation.

We cannot wait until someone comes along to complete us, to give our lives form and substance. That is something that we need to do for ourselves. Then, when someone does come along, they will find a whole, harmonized being waiting for them!

Look to your own spiritual cultivation and allow your friends to look to theirs. In this way you will meet in the center and benefit from each other's cultivation.

This vision of unity and joyful diversity can empower us to live a life of harmonious and exciting engagement.

By being aware and sensitive to the balance and the subtle

shifts of our own yin and yang qualities, we are better able to make proper decisions and conduct ourselves with greater integrity and foresight in our dealings with others.

If you are in a relationship where one person tends to be the dominant or yang energy much of the time, try switching roles for a time. If you are used to deferring many decisions to your partner, try being the one to make the decisions. If your partner tends to take the dynamic leader position in your relationship allow yourself to be the leader for a time. You will, of course, need your partner's cooperation with this. But it will be an interesting practice, both for you and your partner.

The key to happiness is to remain flexible and open-minded. In this way we are always open to new ideas and new experiences and, at the same time, we have a deeper appreciation of what we have.

Friendships and love affairs all come and go. But if you want something to last you give deeply of yourself. You must dig down into the very deepest part of your soul and offer forth the shining pearl that you are.

The art of life is more like navigation than warfare, for what is important is to understand the winds, the tides, the currents, the seasons, and the principles of growth and decay, so that one's actions may use them and not fight them.

ALAN WATTS

Remember the Taoist idea of
"leading from behind"?
One does not always have to
be in the leadership position
to achieve satisfaction.

The opposites have a vital need for each other,
just as no human being can live fully without
relationships—to attempt to do so is either to
stagnate or to court mental and spiritual malaise.

ELLEN CHEN

That everything has its opposite, and that these opposites are the mutual causation of each other, form a basic part of Chuang Tzu's philosophy and later Chinese philosophy. It is important to note that opposites are presented not as irreconcilable conflicts but as complements.

WING-TSIT CHAN

Do not meet a yang force with a yang force.
It will only make matters worse.
To put out a fire use water, not more fire!

Force is followed by loss of strength.

This is not the way of Tao.

LAO TZU

When feeling attacked, if you respond with defensiveness or a return attack, things will only escalate. Try deflecting the attack with a soft, yin approach. Instead of fueling the argument, try backing off.

Instead of trying to make the other person wrong, admit your own mistakes right away.
This doesn't mean caving in to another's unrealistic demands, only that you are taking the time to see the other person's side of things.

Sometimes small problems have a way of growing. It is in being able to discern what is a small but important problem from what is actually insignificant, even if it is slightly irritating, that will save a lot of stress in your relationships.

By not taking the time to notice the small, unimportant problems you will not have to take the time to forgive the other person. This is a much higher level of cultivation.

The "emotional simpleton" is one who is slow to respond to a challenge. In this way she may look foolish to others but, in truth, she is wise. The one who is quick to jump on any simple slight or imaginary offense will prove to be the truly foolish one.

Being an "emotional simpleton" is using the wisdom of foolishness. It is using your intelligence to appear as though you don't even notice the small mistakes and slights of your partner.

An "emotional simpleton" is not sensitive to unimportant things. An "emotional simpleton" does not know how to complain about unimportant details and does not remember what minor trouble people have caused.

By learning this small skill of being an "emotional simpleton" and applying it in the correct instance, you will have the entire world for your spiritual joy, privacy, and cultivation.

HUA CHING NI

If you find yourself having the same negative emotions over and over again, instead of blaming your partner, look at yourself and see where these feelings could be coming from. Remember, oftentimes emotions can be caused by energetic or physiological imbalances and should be treated as such.

When you are emotional,
you lose the vision to see
things clearly. You cannot
control your tongue and
might say something that
would destroy the beautiful
picture of your life.

HUA CHING NI

When we are in the midst of an intense emotional state we do not always think, speak, or act correctly. We often say or do things that we regret later. At the same time, we must be able to forgive our partners, if, in the heat of an argument, they too say or do things that they later regret.

When you find yourself in an intense emotional state, stop and breathe deeply from the belly. Take a moment to compose your thoughts and to let your true feelings come through.

To be successful in a relationship one must give up one's idea of a perfect relationship.

To be happy in a relationship one must learn how to be happy without a relationship.

An important part of
relationships is the ability to
let others remain as
individuals. It is better to
remain as separate and
clearly defined individuals.

Do not lose sight of your own individuality when in a serious relationship. Losing one's own identity in another will create problems in the long run.

Know what to take seriously.
Hua Ching Ni suggests
taking the stance of an
"emotional simpleton." By
maintaining this stance
we can learn to overlook
unimportant problems.

Those who learn to be "emotional simpletons" are blessed. They are immune to pain and being wounded in many circumstances, because the situation will correct itself.

HUA CHING NI

By giving permission to make mistakes, to learn about ourselves in real time, to go through periods of confusion and doubt, we will actually strengthen the roots of our relationships.

The real issue is not
women's liberation
or men's liberation
or world liberation,
it is self-liberation.

HUA CHING NI

If you treat your relationships as a spiritual practice you will benefit beyond your expectations.

It is not necessary that you are on the identical spiritual path or religion with your friends, but if there is some sort of spiritual base in your relationships it will be much easier to share the challenges of life.

A good match resembles
well-paired eyes and limbs;
their interdependence
brings about completion
and fulfillment.

HUA CHING NI

Neither yang nor yin is a fixed state
of being. Trying to be more of one
to the exclusion of the other creates
an excess that defeats itself.

CHUNGLIANG AL HUANG

By treating your relationships as an opportunity for self-cultivation you can benefit both yourself and your friends. By looking at your relationships as an opportunity for mutual growth you will all grow together.

The problem is not one of relationships or of staying together or of making friends. In totality, the problem is one of finding the right partner. Even so, the right partner is always in a process of change.

HUA CHING NI

When one person in
the relationship is
ready for change or
growth but the other
is not, the relationship
seldom survives.

An honorable, comfortable friendship cannot be chosen or bought, but can only be earned.

HUA CHING NI

People often have unrealistic expectations about their relationships. They think it will be like the movies or television shows, where all problems are resolved within a specific time frame, with time left over for commercials and coming attractions.

When people love each other consciously, their energies are intentionally consecrated to the good of humanity. This kind of love offering will inspire others.

In today's fast-paced world many people have difficulty finding the time to cultivate themselves, never mind cultivating a relationship. The secret, though, is not quantity but quality. Constancy is the key to a successful practice, a healthy relationship, and long-lasting happiness.

Knowing harmony is constancy.

Knowing constancy is enlightenment.

LAO TZU

Merely staying in a relationship is not good enough. Often people stay together for years in an unhappy and unhealthy state because of the fear of being alone. But being alone and whole is never as damaging as being in constant conflict or outright abuse.

A mutual exchange and sharing of ideas, thoughts, and feelings is the best way to build a relationship.

Sometimes tragedy brings people closer together. Then again, sometimes it drives them apart. In times of great stress it is important not to burden each other overmuch with doubts and demands. By seeking support outside the relationship from friends and family or even professionally, you will be better able to weather the difficult times.

Flexibility, tolerance, emotional, and intellectual openness, and the ability to respect the cycles of others, both emotional and physical, can be the keys to successful friendships.

If we want our relationships to remain vital, interesting, and fun we need to keep the openness and adventuresome qualities of the "young at heart."

Cultivation is often like learning a musical instrument. It takes time, patience, and the willingness to make unpleasant sounds in the beginning.

FRIENDS

Sometimes we are thrown together by circumstance, work situations, school, or a common interest. Most people find that good, long-lasting friendships can be extremely helpful in life.

Besides family and our marriage partner, our most important relationships in our life are with friends. It is our friends that we mostly choose ourselves.

The Chinese word for friend, *you* or *pengyou*, shows two hands pointing in the same direction.

A good friend is worth his or her weight in gold. Old friends don't need any special or fancy occasions to enjoy each other. If there is a deep understanding between two people the simplest things can be most enjoyable.

Good friends can get us through the hard times. Good friends make the good times even better!

The woodcutter wakes up,

The mountain moon is low.

The old fisherman has come to visit.

You throw down your axe,

And I will leave my fishing boat,

We will find somewhere quiet

To sit and talk.

MA CHIH-YUAN

A good friend can
be a teacher, a guide,
and a reflection of
our higher self.

It is said that there are three levels of friendship. The first is the level of casual acquaintance. The second is where there is sharing. The third, considered the most deep, is the level where we trust friends to criticize us.

DENG MING DAO

A good friend is
someone that we
can truly be
ourselves with, in
all our glory and
with all our faults.

When we give out love and respect to those around us that is what we will receive in turn.

HUA CHING NI

Becoming one of the spiritual healing lights,
you provide a model and spiritual influence
for all spiritual beings.
The radiance of your smile, your speech,
your conduct and your way of life,
weaves a cohesive and beneficial medicine
for all sick minds and bodies.

HUA CHING NI

Taoists believe in teaching by example. Become the living embodiment of the ideals you wish to impart to others.

On the Path of Tao we
"lead from behind."
That means we guide
others in a subtle fashion
rather than by shouting
and giving orders.

If your pursuit is the accomplishment of a greater collective goal, then what is most beneficial to the group is also most important to you.

HUA CHING NI

If, in caring for
others, you treat
them as you would
want to be treated,
you can win their
trust and gratitude.

In caring for others and serving heaven

One must always use restraint.

Restraint means giving up one's own ideas.

LAO TZU

To get what you want out of a friendship one must first learn to give that same thing to another.

It is important to remember that, to the
Taoists, everyone in the universe exists in
relationship with everything else. Even for
the solitary type, there can be found a solace
and a satisfaction in realizing and
experiencing, on a root level, this inherent
relationship between all life forms.
No man, or woman, is an island indeed!

We all want to belong. We all have a desire for union. From the infant who always wants to be with his or her parents to the lover who longs for a mate, from the only person who wants a friend to the ascetic who wants to be close to a deity, the desire for union is overwhelming.

DENG MING DAO

440

441

In any long-term friendship things
will change, people will change,
circumstances will change. If you
are able to flow with the

changes, like water flowing through different pathways, you will prosper. If not, your friendship will flounder.

There was an old man who had been born in the state of Yen but had grown up in the state of Ch'u. Upon reaching old age he decided to return to his ancestral home. Her started out, accompanied by several old friends.

As they were passing through the state of Chin his friends decided to play a joke on him. When they came to a large city they told the old man that this was the capital of Yen. The old man looked at the large city in wonder, amazed at how much it had grown since he last saw it.

Once inside the city they came to a shrine and then his friends told him that it was the shrine of his neighborhood. The old man looked at it and breathed out a deep sigh.

They passed a tumbled down hut and said, "This was your father's home." The old man looked at it solemnly, tears welling in his eyes.

Then, when they came to a burial mound, they said, "This is your father's tomb."

Upon seeing this the old man began weeping aloud. His friends began laughing uproariously and said, "We have been joking you all along. We have never left Chin."

The old man was deeply offended by his friend's teasing but didn't say anything. But later, when he did actually reach his home state and see the capital, his neighborhood shrine, his father's house and tomb, he was strangely unmoved.

LIEH TZU

By opening ourselves up
to our friends emotionally
as well as energetically we
also open ourselves up to
being hurt by them.

In the end, say the poets, the love we get is equal to the love we give. The seeds of love, forgiveness, tolerance, respect, and gratitude that we spread throughout our life will be the fruit that will bloom in our last days.

Being a good friend means living
unconditionally. It means not judging but
supporting, not criticizing but honoring.

450

By treating others as we ourselves would like to be treated we ensure that the respect and tolerance we ask from others will be freely given.

When we practice being a spiritual friend to others we can help them on their Way and provide nourishment for our own path.

452

A good friend can help us through the rocky moments of our lives as well as be there to share in the joyful ones.

Being a good
friend to another
can be a spritual
practice on
its own.

The *tai chi* masters say that
to deflect an attack meet
force with emptiness.

This means not being
attached to being right,
to being the winner, to
feeling superior.

If two people argue and one wins and the other loses, does that mean one is right and the other wrong? Or are they both partly right and partly wrong? Or are they both all right and also all wrong?

CHUANG TZU

It is important to remember that we too have the power to hurt the ones we love. When we do inadvertently hurt them, we must be sure to let them know that we are sorry and that we cherish their friendship.

Bibliography

Blofeld, John. *Taoism: The Road to Immortality*. Boston: Shambhala, 1985.

Chan, Wing-Tsit, trans. *The Way of Lao Tzu (Tao-te ching)*. Indianapolis: Bobbs-Merrill, 1963.

Chang, Jolan. *The Tao of Love and Sex*. Dutton.

Chang, Jolan. *The Tao of the Loving Couple*.

Chang, Steven T. *The Tao of Sexology: The Book of Infinite Wisdom*. San Francisco: Tao Publishing, 1986.

Chia, Mantak. *Male Sexual Energy*. Huntington, New York: Healing Tao Books.

Chia, Mantak and Maneewan. *Healing Love Through the Tao: Cultivating Female Sexual Energy*. Huntington, New York: Healing Tao Books.

Chu, Valentin. *The Yin-Yang Butterfly: Ancient Chinese Secrets for Western Lovers*. New York: Putnam, 1993.

Cooper, J.C. *Taoism: The Way of the Mystic*. Wellingborough, Northamptonshire: The Aquarian Press, 1972.

Cooper, J.C. *Yin & Yang: The Taoist Harmony of Opposites*. Wellingborough, Northamptonshire: The Aquarian Press, 1981.

Dunas, Felice with Phillip Goldberg. *Passion Play*. New York: Riverhead Books, 1997.

Ming-Dao, Deng. 365 *Tao: Daily Meditations*. San Francisco: HarperSanFrancisco, 1992.

Ming-Dao, Deng. *Everyday Dao: Living with Balance and Harmony*. San Francisco: HarperSanFrancisco, 1996.

Ni, Hua-Ching. *8,000 Years of Wisdom: Conversations with Taoist Master Ni, Hua Ching*, Book I Los Angeles: The Shrine of the Eternal Breath of Tao and College of Tao and Traditional Chinese Healing, 1983.

Ni, Hua-Ching. *The Book of Changes and The Unchanging Truth*. Los Angeles: The Shrine of the Eternal Breath of Tao and College of Tao and Traditional Chinese Healing, 1983.

Ni, Hua-Ching. *Essence of Universal Spirituality*. Los Angeles: The Shrine of the Eternal Breth of Tao, College of Tao and Traditional Chinese Healing, 1990.

Ni, Hua-Ching. *Moonlight in the Dark Night*. Los Angeles: The Shrine of the Eternal Breth of Tao, College of Tao and Traditional Chinese Healing, 1991.

Reid, Daniel. *The Tao of Health, Sex & Longevity: A Modern Practical Guide to the Ancient Way*. New York: Fireside, 1989.

Roberts, Moss, trans. *Chinese Fairy Tales & Fantasies*. New York: Pantheon Books, 1979.

Watts, Alan, with Al Chung-liang Huang. *Tao: The Watercourse Way*. New York: Pantheon Books, 1975.

Wile, Douglas. *Art of the Bedchamber*. Albany, New York: State University of New York, 1992.

Wong, Eva, trans. *Harmonizing Yin and Yang*. Boston: Shambhala, 1997.

Yip, Wai-Lim, trans. *Chinese Poetry*. Durham, Mass.: Duke University Press, 1997.

Author Biography

Solala Towler is a musican, poet, and teacher. He is editor of *The Empty Vessel, A Journal of Contemporary Taoism*, a magazine with an international subscription and distribution base (www.abodetao.com). He is also author of *A Gathering of Cranes: Bringing the Tao to the West* and *Embarking On the Way: A Guide to Western Taoism*. He is an instructor of Taoist meditation and of several styles of *chi gong*. He has taught classes and seminars all over the U.S. and abroad and is currently President of the National Qigong Association* U.S.A.

Solala leads yearly tours to China to study *chi gong*, and visits Taoist temples and sacred mountains. You can email him at solala@abodetao.com or call (001)-541-345-8854.

Published by MQ Publications Limited
12 The Ivories, 6–8 Northampton Street
London N1 2HY
Tel: 020 7359 2244   Fax: 020 7359 1616
email: mail@mqpublications.com

Text © Solala Towler 2002
Design: Axis Design Editions Ltd

ISBN: 1-84072-311-4

3 5 7 9 0 8 6 4 2

Printed and bound in China